LET'S FIND OUT! GOOD HEALTH

WHAT ARE FATS?

DANIEL E. HARMON

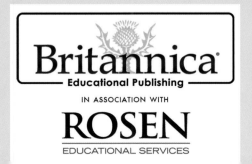

Britannica®
Educational Publishing

IN ASSOCIATION WITH

ROSEN
EDUCATIONAL SERVICES

Published in 2019 by Britannica Educational Publishing (a trademark of Encyclopædia Britannica, Inc.) in association with The Rosen Publishing Group, Inc.
29 East 21st Street, New York, NY 10010

Distributed exclusively by Rosen Publishing.
To see additional Britannica Educational Publishing titles, go to rosenpublishing.com.

First Edition

Britannica Educational Publishing
J.E. Luebering: Executive Director, Core Editorial
Mary Rose McCudden: Editor, Britannica Student Encyclopedia

Rosen Publishing
Kathy Kuhtz Campbell: Senior Editor
Nelson Sá: Art Director
Nicole Russo-Duca: Series Designer and Book Layout
Cindy Reiman: Photography Manager
Nicole DiMella: Photo Researcher

Library of Congress Cataloging-in-Publication Data

Names: Harmon, Daniel E., author.
Title: What are fats? / Daniel E. Harmon.
Description: New York: Britannica Educational Publishing, in Association with Rosen Educational Services, 2019. | Series: Let's find out! Good health | Audience: Grades 1–4. | Includes bibliographical references and index.
Identifiers: LCCN 2017050525| ISBN 9781538302941 (library bound) | ISBN 9781538302958 (pbk.) | ISBN 9781538302965 (6 pack)
Subjects: LCSH: Lipids in human nutrition—Juvenile literature. | Nutrition—Juvenile literature. | Oils and fats—Juvenile literature.
Classification: LCC QP751 .H357 2019 | DDC 613.2/84—dc23
LC record available at https://lccn.loc.gov/2017050525

Manufactured in the United States of America

Photo credits: Cover, back cover, interior pages background Tina Larsson/Shutterstock.com; p. 4 Encyclopædia Britannica, Inc.; p. 5 Fuse/Corbis/Getty Images; p. 6 Charlotte Lake/Shutterstock.com; p. 7 El Nariz/ Shutterstock.com; p. 8 Craevschii Family/Shutterstock.com; p. 9 Wavebreakmedia Ltd/Thinkstock; p. 10 U.S. Food and Drug Administration; p. 11 chombosan/Shutterstock.com; p. 12 Karl Allgaeuer/Shutterstock.com; p. 13 Image Point Fr/Shutterstock.com; p. 14 EdBockStock/Shutterstock.com; p. 15 Science Source/ Getty Images; p. 16 zlikovec/Shutterstock.com; p. 17 Stephan Gladieu/Getty Images; p. 18 Teguh Mujiono/ Shutterstock.com; p. 19 Photographee.eu/Shutterstock.com; p. 20 Dragon Images/Shutterstock.com; p. 21 oliveromg/Shutterstock.com; p. 22 Keith Homan/Shutterstock.com; p. 23 © iStockphoto.com/asiseeit; p. 24 Jupiterimages/Goodshoot/Thinkstock; p. 25 Robert Kneschke/Shutterstock.com; p. 26 Iakov Filimonov/ Shutterstock.com; p. 27 sabza/Shutterstock.com; p. 28 BananaStock/Thinkstock; p. 29 Sergey Novikov/ Shutterstock.com.

CONTENTS

WHY FATS ARE IMPORTANT

News reports, magazine articles, and other sources often warn people about the fats contained in food. Much of the information is disturbing. It is true that some types of fat are unhealthy. Over time, they can lead to dangerous health conditions. Also, fats contain more calories than other nutrients.

Human skin has three layers: the epidermis, the dermis, and a layer made mostly of fat. Body fat stores energy and cushions bones.

VOCABULARY

Nutrients are things that the body needs in order to grow and stay healthy. Fats are nutrients, as are proteins, carbohydrates, minerals, vitamins, and water.

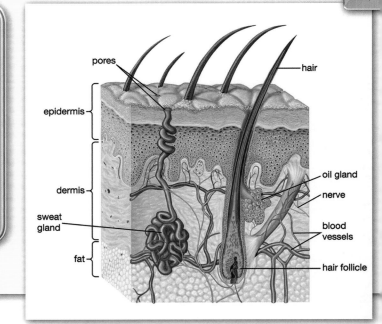

- pores
- hair
- epidermis
- oil gland
- nerve
- dermis
- sweat gland
- blood vessels
- fat
- hair follicle

A boy enjoys a meal of grilled salmon. Salmon is one food that contains healthy fat.

If people eat lots of fatty foods, they may be taking in more calories than they burn.

Not all fats cause problems, though. In fact, fats are necessary. They are part of the normal growth process. They help to produce healthy skin. In addition, the fat stored in the body is a source of energy for times when food is unavailable. Body fat also provides cushioning tissue to protect organs from injury. It helps to keep the body warm in cold weather, too.

It is important to learn which types and amounts of fat are beneficial and which ones can cause harm. Children and adults alike can adopt either healthy or harmful eating habits. They can choose to eat foods that have the right amount of healthy fat. On the other hand, they can choose foods that contain too much fat or unhealthy types of fat.

Where Do Fats Come From?

Fats are substances called lipids. Lipids are found in the cells of living things. They do not dissolve in water. Fats are made up of different molecules, including molecules called fatty acids. Fatty acids are the parts of fats used by the body. When doctors and dieticians speak of fats, they often are talking about fatty acids.

Some fats are solid, not liquid, at room temperature. Solid fats may come from animals or plants. Hundreds of popular foods contain solid

Butter (*left*) is an example of a solid fat. Olive oil (*right*) is an example of a liquid fat.

A man adds olive oil to vegetables while cooking. It is important to learn which forms of fat are healthiest.

fat—for example, dairy products (such as ice cream and butter), cookies, cakes, pastries, pizza, burgers, and hot dogs. Solid fat is also commonly used to cook fried foods, such as French fries and fried chicken.

COMPARE AND CONTRAST

Fats do not dissolve in water. Can you think of common cooking ingredients that do dissolve in water?

Other fats are liquid at room temperature. These fats are called oils. Oils used in cooking often come from olives, corn, soybeans, sunflowers, and safflower. Oil also comes from peanuts and other nuts.

Some fatty acids are necessary to a healthy human diet. Others are less useful to the body. Studying how fats affect human health is a complicated science.

HEALTHY FATS

Humans cannot live without a certain amount of fat in their diet. However, it is important to learn which types of fats are better for health than others. People need to know which foods contain healthful, or "good," fat and which foods contain unhealthful, or "bad," fat.

Fish is one example of a food source containing healthful fat. Some fish are rich in what are called omega-3 fatty acids. Omega-3 fats are especially good for the heart and cardiovascular system. Dieticians

Fish, olives, avocados, certain cooking oils, and nuts are examples of nutritious sources of fat.

A chef pours oil over fresh asparagus spears before roasting them. They will be a healthy side item for a meal.

recommend that people who eat a lot of red meat or poultry replace some of it in their diets with fish and other types of seafood. Avocados, nuts, and tofu are other sources of fats that are mainly beneficial.

Certain oils used in cooking are healthier than others. All cooking oils contain fat. The wisest choices for cooking are olive, sunflower, canola, and peanut oils.

THINK ABOUT IT

Which do you think is healthier— an avocado salad or a hamburger?

HARMFUL FATS

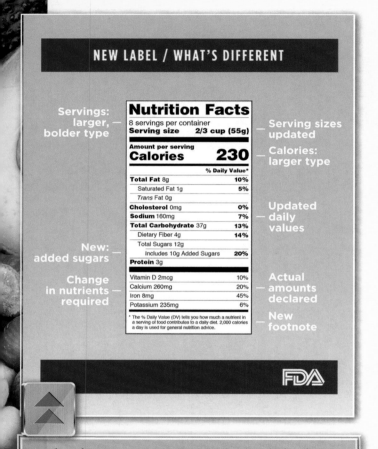

The latest nutrition facts labels show the amounts of different types of fat in packaged foods.

Different foods contain different types of fat. Some are good for human health. Others are dangerous. A problem in the United States is that many of the most popular foods contain the worst kinds of fats.

Harmful fats are contained in snacks such as candy bars, cookies, crackers, pizza, doughnuts, muffins, and potato chips. Also unhealthy in large amounts are the fats found in red meat (beef, pork, lamb), poultry (primarily fried chicken, especially

The body's cardiovascular system is shown in this diagram. Trans fats can cause damage to the cardiovascular system.

▶▶

VOCABULARY

Processed foods are food items that are changed in some way from their original forms before they are packaged and sold.

when fried with the skin), and dairy products (cheese, ice cream, butter).

The category of fatty acids called trans fats are especially bad for the heart and cardiovascular system. They also have been linked to diabetes and other health problems. These "bad" fats are commonly found in packaged baked goods and other processed foods.

Saturated, Unsaturated, and Trans Fats

The main types of fatty acids are saturated, unsaturated (including monounsaturated and polyunsaturated), and trans fats. Moderate amounts of unsaturated fat are necessary for health. Saturated and trans fats are of greatest concern to health professionals.

Fats contain three chemical elements: carbon, hydrogen, and oxygen. The difference between saturated and unsaturated fats depends on the amount of hydrogen. Saturated fats are usually solid at room temperature. Most saturated fats are found in foods that come from animal sources. Examples are red meat, lard, whole milk, cheese, and

Foods from animal sources contain saturated fats, which can cause health problems.

Almonds and other nuts are more nutritious snack choices than items such as potato chips and cookies.

COMPARE AND CONTRAST

How are trans fats and saturated fats similar? How are they different?

butter. Coconut oil is a plant source of saturated fat.

Unsaturated fats are usually liquid at room temperature. Monounsaturated fats are the healthiest fats. Olive, peanut, and canola oils are sources of monounsaturated fats. So are nuts and avocados. Polyunsaturated fats are mainly found in fish. Other sources of polyunsaturated fats include oils from corn, soybeans, and safflower, as well as sesame, sunflower, and flax seeds.

Most trans fats are produced through food processing. Hydrogen is added to vegetable oil, making it become solid at room temperature. This process is called hydrogenation. Food products made with trans fats stay fresh longer on supermarket shelves. However, trans fats are the unhealthiest fats.

Dangers of Too Much Fat

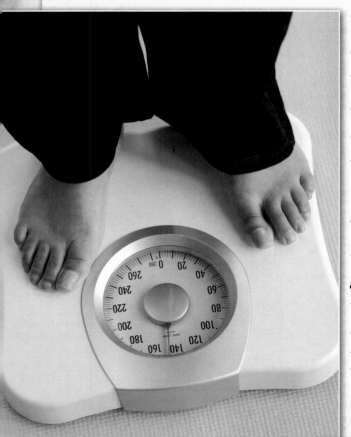

The fats that people eat are different from fat that builds up in their body. However, eating a lot of fatty food can cause people to build up fat in their body and to gain weight. Extreme fat storage leads to obesity. People who are even moderately overweight are at greater risk of health problems than people at normal weight. Obese people face serious health hazards.

Keeping track of weight can alert a person to the possibility of becoming overweight or obese.

An artery can become dangerously blocked by fatty material if a person has an unhealthy diet.

Masses of fat surrounding the heart and arteries force the heart to work harder to pump blood throughout the body. Over time, this condition can lead to heart and circulatory diseases.

COMPARE AND CONTRAST

The two ways to limit or reduce excess fat are to control eating habits and to exercise. Think of exercises that strengthen muscles and combat fat in different areas of the body.

A woman with type 2 diabetes checks the level of glucose in her bloodstream by using a glucose meter. Glucose is a sugar that the body gets from food and uses for energy.

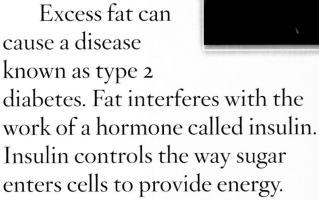

Students work out with light weights in an exercise class. Regular exercise can help people to maintain a healthy weight.

Excess fat can cause a disease known as type 2 diabetes. Fat interferes with the work of a hormone called insulin. Insulin controls the way sugar enters cells to provide energy.

A fat buildup in the liver can cause damage or liver failure. Fat also may be linked to some cancers.

Doctors point out that the greatest health risks result from too much extra fat above the hips. Abdominal obesity can damage vital organs and systems.

FAT AND CHOLESTEROL

Good vs Bad Cholesterol

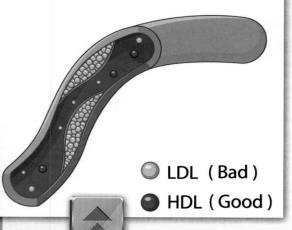

- ● LDL (Bad)
- ● HDL (Good)

This illustration shows how bad cholesterol can clog arteries and restrict the flow of blood.

Many people who worry about their weight focus on two areas of concern in their diet: fat and cholesterol. Some believe the two are the same or are closely related. They think that controlling their fat level also controls their cholesterol level. In reality, the two are quite different, but they affect each other.

Cholesterol is a substance similar to fat. It occurs naturally in humans and other animals. It helps to build healthy cells.

The saturated fats in burgers and fries can raise levels of bad cholesterol.

THINK ABOUT IT

Why is it important to understand the relationships between different types of fats and different types of cholesterol?

Substances called lipoproteins carry cholesterol through the bloodstream. There are two types of lipoproteins, LDLs and HDLs. Doctors call the cholesterol carried by LDLs "bad cholesterol." If not controlled, this cholesterol can clog arteries and cause serious heart problems.

The human body makes all the cholesterol it needs. However, cholesterol also is found in some foods, including egg yolks. The cholesterol in food is called dietary cholesterol. Eating saturated and trans fats raises levels of bad cholesterol more than dietary cholesterol does.

FAT AND CALORIES

A common misunderstanding is the relationship between fats and calories. Calories enter the body through three types of nutrients: fats, carbohydrates, and proteins. Fats contain more than twice as many calories as carbohydrates and proteins. That fact is why some people think dietary fats cause weight gain. Some low-fat and fat-free foods are low in calories, but many are not.

VOCABULARY

Calories are measures of energy, not weight. Calories are burned, or used by the body, during activity. That means that a person's average level of activity helps to determine how many calories the person should take in each day.

A woman uses a smartphone app to check the number of calories in her salad ingredients.

20

Regular exercise is as important as eating balanced meals for preventing weight and health problems.

Many people "count calories" each day. They assume that if they cut down on the calories they eat, they will reduce their body fat. Actually, reducing calories alone may not reduce fat storage. Exercise plays a key role as well.

People need a certain number of calories every day to furnish their bodies with energy. The body uses some calories for its regular functions. Exercise burns additional calories. The number of calories people need depends partly on the amount of exercise they get.

Reducing the Fat Content in Food

During the past few decades, health professionals have warned people against eating too many fatty foods. They have explained the dangers of unhealthy types of fat, especially trans fat. As a result, the public has demanded that food providers offer low-fat or reduced-fat products.

Makers of processed foods have responded. They have found ways to reduce the fat content in dairy products and other fatty foods. However, consumers must compare food products carefully. Claims on food packages may be misleading.

Reduced-fat and skim milk have become common choices over whole milk among many grocery shoppers.

A shopper reads the nutrition facts label of a food product. It is smart to consider fat content when buying food.

Researchers have discovered that some low-fat foods contain many times more sugar than regular products.

Dieticians recommend that shoppers select food with low amounts of fat. Food can be labeled as low fat if it has 3 grams (0.1 ounce) of fat or less

COMPARE AND CONTRAST

Compare the labels on two food products. Note the fat, sugar, and calorie counts for each.

for every 100 calories. For example, people can choose skim milk or reduced-fat milk rather than whole milk. They can buy broth-based rather than cream-based soups. They can choose mustard instead of mayonnaise and salsa instead of cheese dip.

FATS AND FASTING

Some people who are overweight or obese turn to an extreme method of shedding fat. They skip meals. Sometimes they refuse to eat for days at a time. This course of action is called fasting. Fasting can result in short-term weight loss. However, dieticians warn that most people who fast return to their earlier eating habits. In some cases, they gain back their lost weight or even more.

When a person fasts, the first form of weight that the body loses is water. Water loss is not permanent weight loss. The water

A carrot stick is a healthful snack. Dieticians caution against consuming too little fat, however.

has to be replaced in the body eventually. A person who does not have enough water inside the body can become dehydrated. This condition can be dangerous and even fatal.

During a fast, the body loses muscle tissue as well as fat tissue. Meanwhile, it loses essential nutrients. This can weaken the person's immune system. It also can upset their chemical balance and metabolism.

People should drink adequate amounts of water daily to prevent dehydration.

ASK QUESTIONS, EAT SMART

In recent years, food processing companies have provided important information on packaging labels. These details tell how many vitamins and nutrients, if any, the food inside contains. Children may not understand some of the terms and statistics shown on the labels. An adult can explain the most important nutritional values.

The more questions young people ask about what they eat, the smarter they will become about food. For starters, dieticians suggest overall eating habits that can

This mom is teaching her daughter how to read and understand the nutrition facts labels on food items.

A watermelon is a safe form of snack because it contains no harmful ingredients.

help children as well as adults stay healthy.

For example, eat fast food such as burgers, fries, and shakes only occasionally. Choose menu items that are not fried. For snacks, choose such treats as vegetables, fruits, nuts (unsalted or lightly salted), and olives rather than crackers and candy. Drink low-fat or fat-free milk instead of whole milk.

Finally, eat smaller meals. Focus on foods that are known to be rich in vitamins, protein, and other important substances. Eat at regular times, not while trying to do something else. Eat slowly.

THINK ABOUT IT

Why should people base their eating habits on a balanced diet—one that includes a healthy portion of fats as well as other nutrients?

A Balancing Act

When people realize they are overweight, they often try one of the popular diets they see advertised online, on television, or in magazines. The authors of most diets promise that people can enjoy full servings of delicious food and still lose weight. They say certain types of foods are OK to eat and others (especially fatty foods) are bad.

However, most young people do not need a strict diet plan. They need to know the different nutrients that the body requires and the foods

A Cornish game hen with a sizeable salad makes a tasty and healthy meal for this girl.

Health specialists remind children, "Go outside and play, every day." It is important for controlling fat buildup.

that contain each nutrient. Fat is one of the nutrients. It is important for good health.

Keeping a healthy weight is a balancing act. The way to solve dietary problems is not by keeping close counts of fats, calories, or cholesterol. The challenge for everyone is to make wise, basic food choices and to exercise each day.

THINK ABOUT IT

What are some of the popular diets in the news today? Why is it best to avoid these diets and simply adopt smart eating habits every day?

GLOSSARY

cardiovascular Relating to the heart and blood vessels.

cell The tiny, basic building block of living things.

circulatory The system through which blood moves throughout the body.

complicated Difficult or complex.

dehydrated Endangered by a loss of water from the body.

diabetes A condition resulting from too little insulin in the body.

dietary Relating to a diet or the rules of a diet.

dietician A health professional who studies and advises people about their diets and nutritious meals.

hormone A chemical that tells cells and body parts to do certain things.

lipoprotein A type of protein that combines a lipid with a simple protein.

liver The organ that produces bile and causes changes in the blood.

metabolism Process by which substances in cells are built up or broken down.

molecule The smallest unit of a substance that has all the properties of that substance.

obesity The condition of being extremely overweight.

protein A substance that consists of chains of amino acids.

statistics A collection of numbers.

FOR MORE INFORMATION

Books

Are You What You Eat? A Guide to What's on Your Plate and Why! New York, NY: DK Publishing, 2015.

Dickmann, Nancy. What You Need to Know About Obesity (Fact Finders). North Mankato, MN: Capstone Press, 2016.

Hawley, Ella. Exploring Food and Nutrition (Let's Explore Life Science). New York, NY: PowerKids Press, 2013.

Paris, Stephanie Herweck. Straight Talk: The Truth About Food (TIME for Kids). Huntington Beach, CA: Teacher Created Materials, 2013.

Pelkki, Jane Sieving. Healthy Eating (A True Book). New York, NY: Children's Press/Scholastic Inc., 2017.

Schuh, Mari C. Sugars and Fats (What's on MyPlate?). Mankato, MN: Capstone Press, 2013.

Ventura, Marne. 12 Tips for a Healthy Diet (Healthy Living). Mankato, MN: 12-Story Library, 2017.

Websites

ChooseMyPlate.gov
https://www.choosemyplate.gov/kids
Facebook and Twitter: @MyPlate

KidsHealth.org
http://kidshealth.org/en/kids/fat.html

PBSKids.org
http://pbskids.org/games/healthy-habits

Women's and Children's Health Network
http://www.cyh.com/HealthTopics/HealthTopicCategories.aspx?&p=284

INDEX